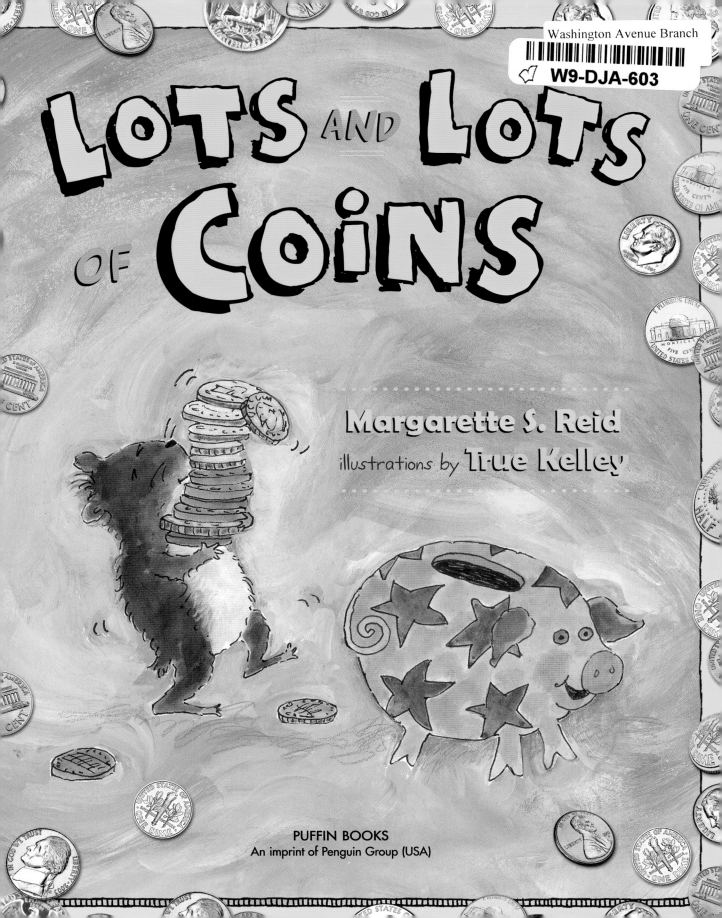

LOTS AND LOTS OF COINS

Margarette S. Reid

illustrations by True Kelley

PUFFIN BOOKS
An imprint of Penguin Group (USA)

To my grandsons, Justin and David,
and their dad, Dave
M.S.R.

For Ronan and Torlis
T.K.

PUFFIN BOOKS
An imprint of Penguin Young Readers Group
Published by the Penguin Group
Penguin Group (USA)
375 Hudson Street
New York, New York 10014, U.S.A.

USA / Canada / UK / Ireland / Australia / New Zealand / India / South Africa / China
Penguin Books Ltd, Registered Offices: 80 Strand, London WC2R 0RL, England

For more information about the Penguin Group visit www.penguin.com

First published in the United States of America by Dutton Children's Books,
a division of Penguin Young Readers Group, 2011
Published by Puffin Books, an imprint of Penguin Young Readers Group, 2013

Text copyright © Margarette S. Reid, 2011
Illustrations copyright © True Kelley, 2011

United States Golden Dollar coin obverse featuring Sacagawea © 1999 United States Mint.
All Rights Reserved. Used with permission.
United States coin images courtesy United States Mint. Used with permission.

THE LIBRARY OF CONGRESS HAS CATALOGED THE DUTTON CHILDREN'S BOOKS EDITION AS FOLLOWS:
Reid, Margarette S.
Lots and lots of coins / by Margarette S. Reid ; illustrated by True Kelley.—1st ed.
p. cm.
Includes bibliographical references.
ISBN 978-0-525-47879-9 (hardcover)
1. Coins—Collectors and collecting—Juvenile literature. 2. Coins—Juvenile literature. I. Kelley, True, ill.
II. Title. CJ89.R39 2010 737.4—dc22 2009053286

Puffin Books ISBN 978-0-14-751059-4

Manufactured in China

1 3 5 7 9 10 8 6 4 2

The publisher does not have any control over and does not
assume any responsibility for author or third-
party websites or their content.

ALWAYS LEARNING   PEARSON

My dad carries paper money in his wallet to buy things. When he spends paper money he usually gets change back. He does this a lot and so we have plenty of coins to look at together.

Are you a collector?

May I see the change?

Dad and I think coins are cool. He's a coin collector. I learn a lot about coins from him.

Dad says coins have been around for a long time—hundreds of years, even thousands of years. Once Dad made me laugh. He emptied a pocketful of beads and shells. That's what people used to use for money.

SOME THINGS PEOPLE USED FOR MONEY

Tobacco—the official money of Virginia and Maryland 1600s–1700s

Cowrie shells—used 3,500 years ago in China and up to 1935 in rural Nigeria!

Oxen (early Greeks)

Bear teeth

Horses—12th-century England

Camels

Wampum beads

Salt (used to preserve food)

Dried fish

Nails (early European Americans)

Fishhooks

Sheep (Egypt and Crete)

Tea leaves

Animal skins

Coiled feather money (Solomon Islands) glued to bark—took 300 birds to make one coil!

Boar's tusk

Coins from around the world come in different shapes and sizes. Dad has a Japanese coin that has a hole right in the center.

Japanese 50 yen coin

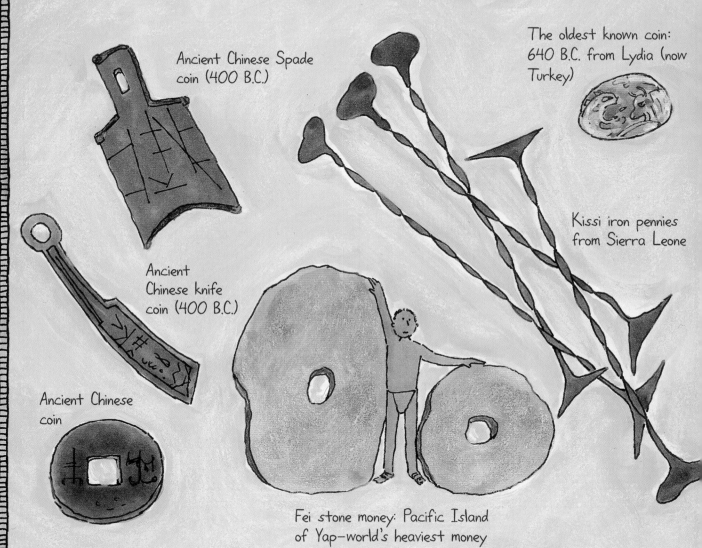

Ancient Chinese Spade coin (400 B.C.)

The oldest known coin: 640 B.C. from Lydia (now Turkey)

Kissi iron pennies from Sierra Leone

Ancient Chinese knife coin (400 B.C.)

Ancient Chinese coin

Fei stone money: Pacific Island of Yap—world's heaviest money

I look for shiny new coins. Dad looks for rare old coins. If a coin is shiny and bright, it is probably new. If it is dull and dark, it is probably old and may be getting valuable.

Dull

Bright

Dad doesn't spend the coins he collects. He fits those into a special folder to protect them. Printed on the folder is the year the coin was struck at the mint.

"That's its birthday," he says. I laugh. I think it is funny to say that coins have birthdays.

"What does 'struck at the mint' mean, Dad? I thought a mint was red-and-white-striped candy!"

Dad smiles. "The mint is where coins are made."

1928 1929 1930 1932 1933 1934 1935

The first U.S. Mint facility in Philadelphia, 1792.

The U.S. Mint facility at Philadelphia, today. There are also United States Mint facilities in Denver, San Francisco, and West Point.

Look for the mint mark on a coin.
D=Denver, S=San Francisco, P=Philadelphia, W=West Point.

Plain, round metal disks are put in a powerful machine. It *strikes* two different pictures into the metal.

One side is called heads, and the other side is called tails.

Flipping a coin is one way to decide who gets the first turn.

Dad says if a mistake is made at the mint, an odd coin may become a treasure to collectors.

The three-legged 1937 buffalo nickel could be worth thousands!

Struck off-center: a coin is worth more with a readable date and mint mark.

A 1955 penny: double printed could be worth $12,000!

This penny was clipped off at the mint.

A penny with a nickel printed on top.

Coins are different colors, depending on the metal used to make them.

 Penny

COPPER

 1974 Uncirculated Penny, made from Aluminum

ALUMINUM

 1849 Liberty Head Dollar

GOLD

Dime

SILVER

600 B.C. Lydian coin

ELECTRUM

 1684 Tin Farthing (British)

TIN

Electrum is a mix of gold and sliver.

After we finish checking for special coins, Dad puts the rest of the change in an old fishbowl. I call it my coin collection. I stir those coins and look through the glass at them, all mixed up.

When I look at my coins, it's fun to pretend I'm rich, but I've found out that it takes a whole lot of change to buy a soccer ball or a hamster at the pet store. You have to save up for the things you really want.

Dad and I make a game of sorting coins by size. I close my eyes and pick a coin out of the fishbowl.

First, I find a penny. A penny is also called a cent.

The Abraham Lincoln penny was issued in 1909 to celebrate the 100th anniversary of his birth.

. THE PENNY .

· HEADS ·   · TAILS ·

The United States Mint produces over a thousand pennies a second.

The Lincoln Memorial, Washington, D.C.

It takes one hundred pennies to buy something that costs one dollar.

LIBERTY

IN GOD WE TRUST

1993 D

VDB

Look for the tiny letters VDB. They are the initials of the artist Victor David Brenner.

Next, I find a smaller, thinner coin. It's a dime. Ten dimes equal a dollar.

Equal is an important word. It means that different things have the same value.

President Franklin Roosevelt

. THE DIME .

· HEADS · · TAILS ·

The dime is the smallest coin we use today.

Olive and oak branches, flaming torch.

PIGGY BANK · FACTS ·

10¢ = 1 dime

THE DIME GAME

Place dimes in this pattern. Make the triangle point up (instead of down) by moving only three dimes.

ONE DIME ONE DIME ONE DIME ONE DIME
ONE DIME ONE DIME ONE DIME
ONE DIME ONE DIME
ONE DIME

=

A quarter is bigger. It takes four quarters to equal one dollar.

President George Washington

e pluribus unum means "one of many"
(many peoples=one nation)

. THE QUARTER .

· HEADS ·   · TAILS ·

George Washington did not
want his face on a coin.
He thought it would make
him look like a king.

PIGGY BANK
· FACTS ·
25¢ = 1 quarter

I feel around for the biggest coin. It's called a half-dollar. It takes two half-dollars to equal a whole dollar.

50¢   50¢

=

THE UNITED STATES OF AMERICA   ONE DOLLAR

The Presidential Seal

. THE HALF-DOLLAR .

· HEADS ·   · TAILS ·

The Kennedy half-dollars were first released in 1964 and were over 90% silver.

President John F. Kennedy

The eagle faces the symbol of peace, olive branches. In his other claw are arrows, representing war.

PIGGY BANK · FACTS ·
50¢ = 1 half-dollar

DESIGN YOUR OWN COIN!

Trace around a half-dollar and then draw your design.

AWESOMENESS

LIBERTY IN GOD WE TRUST 1969

UNITED STATES OF AMERICA 100 DOLLARS

Dad says, "Coins are like a piece of history you can hold in your hand."

New nickels celebrated the anniversary of the purchase of the western lands.

President Thomas Jefferson sent Lewis and Clark to explore the West. One nickel shows how they traveled by keelboat.

Captain Lewis designed the boat that is shown on this coin himself! It was 55 feet long and could be rowed, sailed, towed from the riverbank, or poled like a raft.

WESTWARD JOURNEY
KEELBOAT NICKEL
· 2004 ·

Another shows the peace medal they gave to the Indian people they met.

WESTWARD JOURNEY
PEACE MEDAL
NICKEL
· 2004 ·

Another westward journey nickel has the words "O! The joy!" It tells how they felt when they saw the Pacific Ocean for the first time.

Sacagawea, who guided the Lewis and Clark Expedition, took her baby along. They are on a gold-colored dollar coin.

Baby Jean Baptiste was called "Pomp." He was 3 months old at the start of the trip.

Sacagawea means "Bird Woman."

SACAGAWEA GOLDEN DOLLAR
· 2000–Present ·

Sacagawea was a young Shoshone woman. The expedition she lead took sixteen months!

Dad's collection has other dollar coins, too.

Susan B. Anthony fought to get women the right to vote, although she never got to vote herself.

SUSAN B ANTHONY DOLLAR

· 1979–1981, 1999 ·

The coin was unpopular because its size was easily confused with a quarter.

VOTES FOR WOMEN

HOW LONG MUST WOMEN WAIT FOR LIBERTY?

WOMAN SUFFRAGE

Almost every day we find new state quarters in Dad's pocket change. Each state quarter has a different design to show what that state is proud of. It also tells the year that state became a part of our country.

ACTUAL SIZE

George Washington is on the front of the state quarters.

There are a lot of different presidents on coins. At school we learn about the ones who helped found our country.

PRESIDENTIAL DOLLARS

· 2007–Present ·

In 2007, the U.S. Mint began a new series of one-dollar coins. Each coin features a president, starting with George Washington. Four new coins are made each year.

James Madison

Thomas Jefferson

John Adams

George Washington

"Hey," I tell Dad, "all those Founding Fathers had long hair." I put their coins in one pile.

Abraham Lincoln goes in a different pile. He wore a beard.

All my pennies have Abraham Lincoln's picture on the front, but they have different pictures on the back. The first Lincoln pennies have a picture of wheat sheaves on the back. Then came a different picture—the Lincoln Memorial. The newest change shows four different times in Lincoln's life.

I sort the pennies by the design on the back.

Was I the only president with a beard?

Some rare coins are worth a lot of money. Founding Father Benjamin Franklin's designs were used on the first penny authorized by the United States Congress. I wanted to see that penny, but Dad didn't have one. He said that penny is worth more than a thousand dollars now.

One thousand dollars! ($1,000!) That's one hundred thousand pennies! (100,000!)

Fugio means "time flies"

13 linked circles represent the 13 colonies.

Sundial

"We are one"

· HEADS ·   · TAILS ·

FRANKLIN PENNY (FUGIO CENT)
· 1787 ·

The copper in these coins probably came from the copper bands from powder kegs.

"Mind your business" means build it up to make the U.S. stronger.

A penny saved is a penny earned.
Benjamin Franklin

Sometimes Dad and I have so many coins that we take them to the bank to trade for paper money. We used to count out sets of coins and fill paper tubes with them, but now there are machines that do the counting for us.

I like to see all that money!

I'm glad coins keep changing. That's what makes them so much fun—especially when I collect them with my dad.

AUTHOR'S NOTE

A coin is a piece of history you can hold in your hand. It is exciting to find a lost coin. See a penny. Pick it up. All the day you'll have good luck! Look between the couch cushions and in the washing machine. Did you find a nickel? Does it have a buffalo on it? In 1913 James E. Fraser designed one of the most popular nickels ever minted. It featured an animal that was uniquely American although it no longer roamed the western prairies. James Fraser was acutely aware of this loss and honored both the buffalo and Native Americans with his beautiful design.

A new buffalo design appeared on a nickel in 2006. This time the buffalo faces to the right, not the left. Indeed the buffalo has returned to the lands it once roamed. If you go to your public library, you can become a history sleuth and discover many fun facts about coins. Librarians love to help kids find books on subjects in which they are interested.

A librarian helped the author find a wonderful picture book that tells the story of James E. Fraser and the 1913 buffalo nickel. It is *The Buffalo Nickel* by Taylor Morrison, Houghton Mifflin Company, Boston, Massachusetts, 2002.

She also helped me find these interesting books about coins: *The Coin Counting Book* by Rozanne Lanczak Williams, Charlesbridge Publishing, Watertown, MA, 2001 and *Follow the Money* by Loreen Leedy, Holiday House, Inc., New York, N.Y., 2002.

Every coin ever minted in our country is described in *A Guide Book of United States Coins* by R. S. Yeoman, edited by Kenneth Bressett. It is updated each year. There is also a U.S. Mint web site at http://www.usmint.gov/kids/index/cfm. Here you can find out great facts about coins and even take a tour of the mint!

Coins are a wonderful hobby to share with your family and friends. Be a coin collector. It's fun!

If you collect coins, you are a numismatist! (new-MIZ-mah-tist)

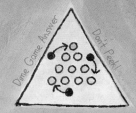

Dime Game Answer   Don't Peek!